CW01430985

POWERFUL PROMISES
— IN THE —
WAR ROOM

DANIEL B LANCASTER

Lightkeeper Books
Nashville, Tennessee

LIGHTKEEPER
BOOKS

LIGHTKEEPER
BOOKS

Copyright © 2018 by Daniel B Lancaster.

All rights reserved.

Powerful Promises in the War Room/ Daniel B Lancaster. –1st ed.

ISBN 978-1980885313

Scriptures marked (CEV) are from Contemporary English Version®
Copyright © 1995 American Bible Society. All rights reserved.

Scriptures marked (ESV) are from The Holy Bible, English Standard
Version® (ESV®) Copyright © 2001 by Crossway, a publishing
ministry of Good News Publishers. All rights reserved.

Scriptures marked (HCSB) are from Holman Christian Standard Bible®
Copyright © 1999, 2000, 2002, 2003, 2009 by Holman Bible Publishers.

Scriptures marked (NASB) are from: NEW AMERICAN STANDARD
BIBLE®, Copyright © 1960,1962,1963,1968,1971,1972,1973,
1975,1977,1995 by The Lockman Foundation. Used by permission.

Scriptures marked (NIV) are from THE HOLY BIBLE, NEW
INTERNATIONAL VERSION®, NIV® Copyright © 1973, 1978, 1984, 2011
by Biblica, Inc.® Used by permission. All rights reserved worldwide.

Scriptures marked (NKJV) are from the New King
James Version®. Copyright © 1982 by Thomas Nelson.
Used by permission. All rights reserved.

Scriptures marked (NLT) are from the Holy Bible, New Living
Translation, copyright © 1996, 2004, 2015 by Tyndale House
Foundation. Used by permission of Tyndale House Publishers,
Inc., Carol Stream, Illinois 60188. All rights reserved.

TO JEFF, NEA, ZACH, BETH, KARIS, AND ZANE

When we walked through the valley of the shadow
of death, you were with us, O Lord

TABLE OF CONTENTS

PREFACE

My prayer is this book will strengthen your walk with God. May you draw closer to Jesus every day and be filled with the Spirit. May you have a deep sense in your spirit that God loves you and will never let you go.

I've also included an excerpt from my bestselling book Powerful Prayers in the War Room. With over 1,500 reviews, God has blessed many through this book and I wanted to give you a chance to "try before you buy."

If you like the book, please leave a review. Your feedback will help other believers find this book easier and encourage me in my calling to write practical, powerful books to encourage, equip, and empower Christians throughout the world.

Every Blessing,

Daniel B Lancaster
Nashville, Tennessee — April 2018

INTRODUCTION

Let God's promises shine on your problems.

- CORRIE TEN BOOM

Satan wants you dead. I'm not trying to scare you. That is just the spiritual reality of the world we live in today. (John 10:10)

And if Satan can't kill you, he will try to destroy your business or family or friendships. That is his goal.

And if the devil can't destroy you, he will try to steal from you. One day, you will wake up and your confidence and joy will be gone. It's happened to me before.

All of us face an uphill battle if we try to defeat Satan on our own. But, God has given us a very powerful weapon again Satan.

God has made powerful promises to you and me that give us the strength and faith to overcome the devil.

Our family of six served as missionaries in Southeast Asia for 12 years and I can tell you from firsthand experience that the promises of God give you the edge you need in spiritual war-fare.

We saw many people come to Christ and follow Him, and it would never have happened if we weren't trusting in the promises of God.

The promises of God have helped me, and many others over-come great challenges in our lives; and I want them to help you too.

If you feel like you're at the end of your rope, please hold on a little longer. The promises of God are going to save the day.

The one-hundred promises in this little book are going to:

- Restore your confidence and joy
- Give you peace and strength
- Increase your faith and love, and
- Bring healing and deliverance to you and your family

After I lost my wife of thirty years to ovarian cancer, my life crumbled. So much grief and sadness. Trying to help my precious children through the loss of their mother, while I was also grieving, overwhelmed me. Everything felt hopeless and dark.

That's when I turned to the powerful promises of God (like I have so many times in my ministry). I clung to the Rock while the Powerful Promises in the War Room

storm raged around me. He carried me and delivered my soul as I walked through the valley of the shadow of death.

No matter where you are today, friend, I believe God's pow-erful promises will also help you. That's why I put together this collection of the one-hundred most powerful promises in God's word.

I also created an audio file of these promises you can listen to as you drive to work, or work around the house, or are spending time in your war room. You can download the audio file here:

go.lightkeeperbooks.com/audiopromise

If you have children or grandchildren, listen to the audio file with them – perhaps right before bedtime or when you are driving to their next activity. God's promises will be one of the best gifts you ever give them.

Let these promises wash over your soul and renew you. Let them restore the joy of your salvation. Let them cleanse and strengthen your heart.

May they draw you closer to the God who always keeps His promises.

1

CONFIDENCE PROMISES

I will give them a heart to know me, that I am the Lord. They will be my people, and I will be their God, for they will return to me with all their heart.

Jeremiah 24:7 (NKJV)

Keep this Book of the Law always on your lips; meditate on it day and night, so that you may be careful to do everything written in it. Then you will be prosperous and successful. Have I not commanded you? Be strong and courageous. Do not be afraid; do not be discouraged, for the Lord your God will be with you wherever you go.

Joshua 1:8-9 (CEV)

It is God who arms me with strength and keeps my way secure. He makes my feet like the feet of a deer; he causes me to stand on the heights.

Psalms 18:32-33 (CEV)

But you are a chosen people, a royal priesthood, a holy nation, God's special possession, that you may declare the praises of him who called you out of darkness into his wonderful light.

1 Peter 2:9 (HCSB)

If anyone is in Christ, the new creation has come: The old has gone, the new is here!

2 Corinthians 5:17 (NASB)

Being confident of this, that he who began a good work in you will carry it on to completion until the day of Christ Jesus.

Philippians 1:6 (NKJV)

Do not let your heart envy sinners, but always be zealous for the fear of the Lord. There is surely a future hope for you, and your hope will not be cut off.

Proverbs 23:17-18 (NKJV)

When you pass through the waters, I will be with you; and when you pass through the rivers, they will not sweep over you. When you walk through the fire, you will not be burned; the flames will not set you ablaze.

Isaiah 43:2 (CEV)

*With your help I can advance against a troop;
with my God I can scale a wall.*

Psalms 18:29 (HCSB)

*For I am convinced that neither death nor life,
neither angels nor demons, neither the present
nor the future, nor any powers, neither height
nor depth, nor anything else in all creation,
will be able to separate us from the love of God
that is in Christ Jesus our Lord.*

Romans 8:38-39 (NIV)

2

DELIVERANCE PROMISES

For God so loved the world that he gave his one and only Son, that whoever believes in him shall not perish but have eternal life.

John 3:16 (NASB)

Truly I tell you, whoever hears my word and believes him who sent me has eternal life and will not be judged but has crossed over from death to life.

John 5:24 (HCSB)

For he has rescued us from the dominion of darkness and brought us into the kingdom of the Son he loves.

Colossians 1:13 (NASB)

For in the day of trouble he will keep me safe in his dwelling; he will hide me in the shelter of his sacred tent and set me high upon a rock.

Psalms 27:5 (ESV)

I sought the Lord, and he answered me; he delivered me from all my fears.

Psalms 34:4 (NIV)

If you declare with your mouth, "Jesus is Lord," and believe in your heart that God raised him from the dead, you will be saved.

Romans 10:9 (CEV)

Submit yourselves, then, to God. Resist the devil, and he will flee from you.

James 4:7 (HCSB)

The Lord is a refuge for the oppressed, a stronghold in times of trouble. Those who know your name trust in you, for you, Lord, have never forsaken those who seek you.

Psalms 9:9-10 (NLT)

The Lord is good, a refuge in times of trouble. He cares for those who trust in him.

Nahum 1:7 (NLT)

The Lord will rescue me from every evil attack and will bring me safely to his heavenly kingdom. To him be glory for ever and ever. Amen.

2 Timothy 4:18 (NIV)

3

FAITH PROMISES

Jesus replied, "Truly I tell you, if you have faith as small as a mustard seed, you can say to this mountain, 'Move from here to there,' and it will move. Nothing will be impossible for you."

Matthew 17:20 (HCSB)

Call on me in the day of trouble; I will deliver you, and you will honor me.

Psalm 50:15 (NASB)

Blessed is the one who perseveres under trial because, having stood the test, that person will receive the crown of life that the Lord has promised to those who love him.

James 1:12 (NASB)

For no matter how many promises God has made, they are "Yes" in Christ. And so through him the "Amen" is spoken by us to the glory of God.

2 Corinthians 1:20 (NKJV)

For no word from God will ever fail.

Luke 1:37 (NKJV)

For the Lamb at the center of the throne will be their shepherd; he will lead them to springs of living water. And God will wipe away every tear from their eyes.

Revelation 7:17 (HCSB)

I have been crucified with Christ and I no longer live, but Christ lives in me. The life I now live in the body, I live by faith in the Son of God, who loved me and gave himself for me.

Galatians 2:20 (NLT)

The thief comes only to steal and kill and destroy; I have come that they may have life and have it to the full.

John 10:10 (CEV)

You make known to me the path of life; you will fill me with joy in your presence, with eternal pleasures at your right hand.

Psalms 16:11 (NASB)

Jesus said to her, "I am the resurrection and the life. The one who believes in me will live, even though they die."

John 11:25 (NLT)

4

HEALING PROMISES

But he was pierced for our transgressions, he was crushed for our iniquities; the punishment that brought us peace was on him, and by his wounds we are healed.

Isaiah 53:5 (NLT)

And I will do whatever you ask in my name, so that the Father may be glorified in the Son. You may ask me for anything in my name, and I will do it.

John 14:13-14 (NKJV)

For thus says the One who is high and lifted up, who inhabits eternity, whose name is Holy: "I dwell in the high and holy place, and also with him who is of a contrite and lowly spirit, to revive the spirit of the lowly, and to revive the heart of the contrite and of the lowly and to revive the heart of the contrite."

Isaiah 57:15 (ESV)

He heals the brokenhearted and binds up their wounds.

Psalms 147:3 (ESV)

If my people, who are called by my name, will humble themselves and pray and seek my face and turn from their wicked ways, then I will hear from heaven, and I will forgive their sin and will heal their land. Now my eyes will be open and my ears attentive to the prayers offered in this place.

2 Chronicles 7:14-15 (NLT)

If we confess our sins, he is faithful and just and will forgive us our sins and purify us from all unrighteousness.

1 John 1:9 (ESV)

The righteous cry out, and the Lord hears them; he delivers them from all their troubles.

Psalms 34:17 (NKJV)

Then your light will break forth like the dawn, and your healing will quickly appear; then your righteousness will go before you, and the glory of the Lord will be your rear guard. Then you will call, and the Lord will answer; you will cry for help, and he will say: Here am I. If you do away with the yoke of oppression, with the pointing finger and malicious talk.

Isaiah 58:8-9 (NKJV)

This is the confidence we have in approaching God: that if we ask anything according to his will, he hears us. And if we know that he hears us—whatever we ask—we know that we have what we asked of him.

1 John 5:14-15 (NASB)

Therefore, confess your sins to each other and pray for each other so that you may be healed. The prayer of a righteous person is powerful and effective.

James 5:16 (CEV)

5

LIFE PROMISES

The Lord appeared to us in the past, saying: I have loved you with an everlasting love; I have drawn you with unfailing kindness.

Jeremiah 31:3 (ESV)

If you love me, you will do what I have said, and my Father will love you. I will also love you and show you what I am like.

John 14:21 (CEV)

But from everlasting to everlasting the Lord's love is with those who fear him, and his righteousness with their children's children.

Psalms 103:17 (NKJV)

I will be glad and rejoice in your love, for you saw my affliction and knew the anguish of my soul.

Psalms 31:7 (CEV)

When I said, my foot is slipping, your unfailing love, Lord, supported me. When anxiety was great within me, your consolation brought me joy.

Psalms 94:18-19 (NASB)

But seek first his kingdom and his righteousness, and all these things will be given to you as well.

Matthew 6:33 (CEV)

God made him who had no sin to be sin for us, so that in him we might become the righteousness of God.

2 Corinthians 5:21 (HCSB)

Every good and perfect gift is from above, coming down from the Father of the heavenly lights, who does not change like shifting shadows.

James 1:17 (NIV)

Through these he has given us his very great and precious promises, so that through them you may participate in the divine nature, having escaped the corruption in the world caused by evil desires.

2 Peter 1:4 (NLT)

For the Lord God is a sun and shield; the Lord bestows favor and honor; no good thing does he withhold from those whose walk is blameless.

Psalms 84:11 (NIV)

6

PEACE PROMISES

You will keep in perfect peace those whose minds are steadfast, because they trust in you.

Isaiah 26:3 (NIV)

Blessed is the one who trusts in the Lord, whose confidence is in him. They will be like a tree planted by the water that sends out its roots by the stream. It does not fear when heat comes; its leaves are always green. It has no worries in a year of drought and never fails to bear fruit.

Jeremiah 17:7-8 (NLT)

Peacemakers who sow in peace reap a harvest of righteousness.

James 3:18 (NIV)

I have told you these things, so that in me you may have peace. In this world you will have trouble. But take heart! I have overcome the world.

John 16:33 (ESV)

Because of the Lord's great love, we are not consumed, for his compassions never fail. They are new every morning; great is your faithfulness.

Lamentations 3:22-23 (NLT)

Cast all your anxiety on him because he cares for you.

1 Peter 5:7 (CEV)

Do not be anxious about anything, but in every situation, by prayer and petition, with thanksgiving, present your requests to God. And the peace of God, which transcends all understanding, will guard your hearts and your minds in Christ Jesus.

Philippians 4:6-7 (NASB)

In peace I will lie down and sleep, for you alone, Lord, make me dwell in safety. Psalms 4:8 (CEV) Peace I leave with you; my peace I give you. I do not give to you as the world gives. Do not let your hearts be troubled and do not be afraid.

John 14:27 (NIV)

Trust in the Lord with all your heart and lean not on your own understanding; in all your ways submit to him, and he will make your paths straight.

Proverbs 3:5-6 (HCSB)

7

POWER PROMISES

Ah, Sovereign Lord, you have made the heavens and the earth by your great power and outstretched arm. Nothing is too hard for you.

Jeremiah 32:17 (NASB)

And afterward, I will pour out my Spirit on all people. Your sons and daughters will prophesy, your old men will dream dreams, your young men will see visions. Even on my servants, both men and women, I will pour out my Spirit in those days.

Joel 2:28-29 (HCSB)

Because you are his sons, God sent the Spirit of his Son into your hearts, the Spirit who calls out, "Abba, Father."

Galatians 4:6 (NKJV)

But you will receive power when the Holy Spirit comes on you; and you will be my witnesses in Jerusalem, and in all Judea and Samaria, and to the ends of the earth.

Acts 1:8 (ESV)

For the Spirit God gave us does not make us timid, but gives us power, love and self-discipline.

2 Timothy 1:7 (NKJV)

I will give them an undivided heart and put a new spirit in them; I will remove from them their heart of stone and give them a heart of flesh. Then they will follow my decrees and be careful to keep my laws. They will be my people, and I will be their God.

Ezekiel 11:19-20 (CEV)

If you then, though you are evil, know how to give good gifts to your children, how much more will your Father in heaven give the Holy Spirit to those who ask him!

Luke 11:13 (ESV)

Now the Lord is the Spirit, and where the Spirit of the Lord is, there is freedom. And we all, who with unveiled faces contemplate the Lord's glory, are being transformed into his image with ever-increasing glory, which comes from the Lord, who is the Spirit.

2 Corinthians 3:17-18 (ESV)

Now to him who is able to do immeasurably more than all we ask or imagine, according to his power that is at work within us...

Ephesians 3:20 (HCSB)

May the God of hope fill you with all joy and peace as you trust in him, so that you may overflow with hope by the power of the Holy Spirit.

Romans 15:13 (NLT)

8

PROTECTION PROMISES

God is our refuge and strength, an ever-present help in trouble. Therefore, we will not fear, though the earth gives way and the mountains fall into the heart of the sea, though its waters roar and foam and the mountains quake with their surging.

Psalms 46:1-3 (CEV)

Call on me in the day of trouble; I will deliver you, and you will honor me.

Psalms 50:15 (NLT)

Every word of God is flawless; he is a shield to those who take refuge in him.

Proverbs 30:5 (NIV)

*Even though I walk through the darkest valley,
I will fear no evil, for you are with me; your
rod and your staff, they comfort me.*

Psalms 23:4 (NLT)

*The Lord is my light and my salvation– whom
shall I fear? The Lord is the stronghold of my
life– of whom shall I be afraid?*

Psalms 27:1 (NKJV)

*The name of the Lord is a fortified tower; the
righteous run to it and are safe.*

Proverbs 18:10 (NLT)

*Whoever dwells in the shelter of the Most High
will rest in the shadow of the Almighty.*

Psalms 91:1 (ESV)

*You are my hiding place; you will protect me
from trouble and surround me with songs of
deliverance.*

Psalms 32:7 (NLT)

*The salvation of the righteous comes from the
Lord; he is their stronghold in time of trouble.
The Lord helps them and delivers them; he
delivers them from the wicked and saves them,
because they take refuge in him.*

Psalm 37:39-40 (ESV)

9

PROVISION PROMISES

And my God will meet all your needs according to the riches of his glory in Christ Jesus.

Philippians 4:19 (ESV)

And God is able to bless you abundantly, so that in all things at all times, having all that you need, you will abound in every good work.

2 Corinthians 9:8 (CEV)

Ask me, and I will make the nations your inheritance, the ends of the earth your possession.

Psalms 2:8 (HCSB)

Cast your cares on the Lord and he will sustain you; he will never let the righteous be shaken.

Psalms 55:22 (NKJV)

"For I know the plans I have for you," declares the Lord, "plans to prosper you and not to harm you, plans to give you hope and a future."

Jeremiah 29:11 (NIV)

How abundant are the good things that you have stored up for those who fear you, that you bestow in the sight of all, on those who take refuge in you.

Psalms 31:19 (HCSB)

I was young and now I am old, yet I have never seen the righteous forsaken or their children begging bread.

Psalms 37:25 (ESV)

The poor and needy search for water, but there is none; their tongues are parched with thirst. But I the Lord will answer them; I, the God of Israel, will not forsake them. I will make rivers flow on barren heights, and springs within the valleys. I will turn the desert into pools of water, and the parched ground into springs.

Isaiah 41:17-18 (HCSB)

When hard pressed, I cried to the Lord; he brought me into a spacious place.

Psalms 118:5 (NIV)

*Take delight in the Lord, and he will give you
the desires of your heart.*

Psalms 37:4 (HCSB)

10

STRENGTH PROMISES

Do not fear, for I am with you; do not be dismayed, for I am your God. I will strengthen you and help you; I will uphold you with my righteous right hand.

Isaiah 41:10 (NASB)

But God has chosen the foolish things of the world to put to shame the wise, and God has chosen the weak things of the world to put to shame the things which are mighty; and the base things of the world and the things which are despised God has chosen, and the things which are not, to bring to nothing the things that are, that no flesh should glory in His presence.

1 Corinthians 1:27-29 (NKJV)

No temptation has overtaken you except what is common to mankind. And God is faithful;

he will not let you be tempted beyond what you can bear. But when you are tempted, he will also provide a way out so that you can endure it.

1 Corinthians 10:13 (NIV)

But he said to me, "My grace is sufficient for you, for my power is made perfect in weakness." Therefore, I will boast all the more gladly about my weaknesses, so that Christ's power may rest on me.

2 Corinthians 12:9 (NIV)

Come to me, all you who are weary and burdened, and I will give you rest. Take my yoke upon you and learn from me, for I am gentle and humble in heart, and you will find rest for your souls. For my yoke is easy and my burden is light.

Matthew 11:28-30 (NASB)

I can do all this through him who gives me strength.

Philippians 4:13 (NIV)

In the same way, the Spirit helps us in our weakness. We do not know what we ought to pray for, but the Spirit himself intercedes for us through wordless groans. And he who searches our hearts knows the mind of the Spirit, because the Spirit intercedes for God's people in accordance with the will of God.

Romans 8:26-28 (NKJV)

The Lord is my strength and my shield; my heart trusts in him, and he helps me. My heart leaps for joy, and with my song I praise him.

Psalms 28:7 (NASB)

Surely God is my salvation; I will trust and not be afraid. The Lord, the Lord himself, is my strength and my defense; he has become my salvation.

Isaiah 12:2 (NIV)

But those who hope in the Lord will renew their strength. They will soar on wings like eagles; they will run and not grow weary, they will walk and not be faint.

Isaiah 40:31 (ESV)

CONCLUSION

Jesus said that Satan comes to steal and kill and destroy. You don't live on this earth long to experience the chaos and calamity the devil brings. I know there have been difficult parts to your journey and it makes me sad.

Thankfully, Jesus promised that we would have life, abundant and free. Such good news! And Jesus' death and resurrection assures every believer that God always delivers on His promises.

Many believers have found standing on the promises of God the key to an abundant and victorious Christian life. I know I have.

Each section in this little book gives you ten key promises from God's word. You can stand on the unshakable Rock with these promises.

If you need more peace or confidence – God has promises for you. If you are seeking Him for strength or healing – God has promises for you. Do you need more faith? Again, God is the answer.

Walking through my wife's death was the hardest challenge of my life. God's promises, however, kept me close to Him and gave me the spiritual power to win the battle.

I am so thankful to report that all my children continue to follow and serve the Lord. The death of their mother caused them to draw closer to God and not fall away. Yet another promise from God fulfilled.

So, now it is up to you. Let me challenge you to read these promises often. Download the audio file and listen to them every day for 30 days. Let the promises of God wash, cleanse, and renew your soul. Follow this plan and I can promise your world will look very different very soon.

Lord Jesus,

You are strong and mighty. Nothing is too difficult for you. You made the stars and the sun and the galaxies. You made the mountains and oceans and rivers. Everything on earth has breath from You. And you are making my friend new every day.

Forgive us for relying on our own strength and understanding. Forgive us for being part of the problem, instead of part of the solution. Forgive us for not living our life based on Your promises, but the promises of others.

Lord, help my friend plant these promises deep in their heart. Give them the grace to water and tend the powerful seeds of Your Word as they grow. I pray that in the coming months and years, the promises in this book will produce a great harvest for Your kingdom in their life and the lives of those they love.You are God and we are the sheep of your pasture.

We yearn to follow you and bring you glory, Almighty God.May Your Kingdom come and Your Will be done in my friend's life. May today be the start of a journey that ends on bended knee before Your throne. May Your goodness and kindness follow them all the days of their life.

In Jesus Name,

Amen

THANK YOU

Before you go, I'd like to say "thank you" again for purchasing my book and I hope you have been blessed by it. I know you could have picked from dozens of books, but you felt the Lord leading you to mine.

Again, a big thank you for downloading Powerful Promises in the War Room and reading it to the end.

Could I ask a *small* favor? Could you take a minute to leave a review for this book?

Think of your brief review as giving a short testimony that helps others know if this book is what they need to grow in their spiritual life.

Your review will help me continue to write books that help people grow in their walk with Jesus. And if you loved it, please let me know that too! :>

BONUS

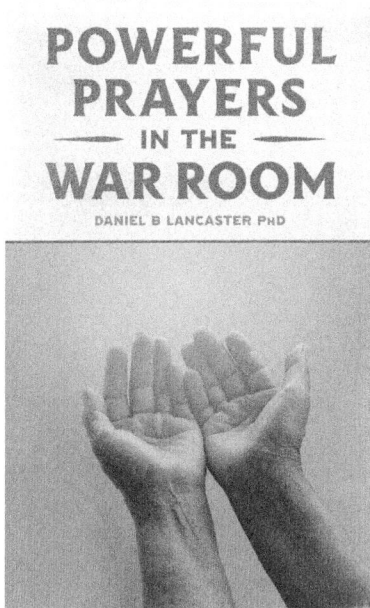

Don't forget to download your free Powerful Prayers Bonus Pak! The free Powerful Prayers Bonus Pak includes three resources to help you pray powerful prayers:

- 100 Promises – Audio Version
- 40 Faith-Building Quotes
- 40 Powerful Prayers.

All are suitable for framing. To download your free Powerful Prayers Bonus Pak go to:

go.lightkeeperbooks.com/powerpak

I've also included an excerpt from my bestselling book Powerful Prayers in the War Room. With over 1,500 reviews, God has blessed many through this book and I wanted to give you a chance to "try before you buy."

INTRODUCTION

The one concern of the devil is to keep Christians from praying. He fears nothing from prayerless studies, prayerless work and prayerless religion. He laughs at our toil, mocks at our wisdom, but he trembles when we pray.

– SAMUEL CHADWICK

This is a simple book on prayer.

You will learn the most important lessons I've gathered about prayer in the last 40 years – principles I wish people had taught me long ago. I'm not as powerful a prayer warrior as I want to be, but the truths I will share with you have helped my prayer life a great deal. The lessons you will learn in this book have helped me, and I believe will help you, too.

For many years, prayer was frustrating and hard for me to do consistently. This was my problem: I wanted to pray, I had been told I should pray, but I didn't know how to pray. When I tried to pray my mind would wander, I found myself bored, and I felt prayer was a complicated exercise I could never master. Just being honest. Conversations with other believers convinced me I wasn't the only one feeling that way about prayer. Earnest followers of Jesus shared similar thoughts.

When our family of six moved to Southeast Asia as missionaries, spiritual warfare became a real issue. Having pastored in America, my prayer life had looked like a roller coaster – some highs, but mostly lows, twists, and turns. Working with national believers for twelve years overseas, I was struck with how they prayed powerful prayers and I didn't. I don't mean emotional prayers; I mean prayers that were answered in ways that brought glory to God and saw His kingdom advance on the earth.

So, I started a journey of learning how to pray. Although I read many books on prayer, my main strategy was to look in the Bible and see how Jesus prayed and what He prayed about during his ministry. Then, I tried to copy Him in a way that would forge a habit. The rest of the book outlines the helpful gems I learned: the four weapons of prayer, seven powerful prayer topics, four ways God answers prayer, three war room prayer strategies, and nine tips to improve your prayer life.

We need powerful prayer warriors in the war room if our world is going to change. Clearly, most of the problems the church faces today are from a lack of prayer. Use this book to learn how to pray better. Use it to teach your children and grandchildren. God has always used the simple things to confound the wise. My prayer is God would use me and you to change the world one more time. Change, I believe, will only come on our knees.

1

FOUR WEAPONS OF POWERFUL PRAYER

When the devil sees a man or woman who really
believes in prayer, who knows how to pray, and
who really does pray, and, above all, when he
sees a whole church on its face before God in
prayer, he trembles as much as he ever did,
for he knows that his day in that church or
community is at an end.

– R.A. TORREY

Many people struggle with knowing how to pray. I know I have through the years. They have heard many times they should pray, but never received the tools to do so. They enter the War Room of prayer empty-handed and soon grow discouraged. They find themselves wishing they could pray better and feeling guilty they don't.

As you enter the War Room, remember Jesus is with you. He is the Great High Priest and knows how to pray perfectly. During his ministry on earth, Jesus showed his disciples how to pray, and he wants to show you how to pray too. Few actions make Jesus happier than when one of his children bow beside him and join him in prayer!

In this section, you will learn four weapons of powerful prayer: praise, repentance, asking, and yielding. Each part is important to a healthy prayer life. If your prayer life is dry or boring, usually the reason is one of the four weapons of prayer is missing. Make each weapon of powerful prayer a habit and watch your prayer life grow.

PRAISE

The right way to pray is to stretch out our hands and ask of One who we know has the heart of a Father.

— DIETRICH BONHOEFFER

Praise is the first weapon in powerful prayer. Each of Jesus' recorded prayers starts with praise and we should copy Him. Luke 10:21 says:

At that very time He rejoiced greatly in the Holy Spirit, and said, "I praise You, O Father, Lord of heaven and earth, that You have hidden these things from the wise and intelligent and have revealed them to infants. Yes, Father, for this way was well-pleasing in Your sight." (NASB)

It makes sense for praise to be the first part of prayer. When we begin to pray, we are ushered into the throne room of Almighty God – with the angels and seraphim. Other believers join us before God's throne. Throughout the Bible, the first response people make in God's presence is worship.

Why is praise a powerful weapon when we pray?

We were created to love God and people, but because of original sin, we found ourselves in circumstances where we hurt others, and others hurt us. Soon we developed the idea our main task was to guard our heart. We built walls to keep others out. Occasionally, we would let someone in, but doing so terrified us, and we soon found a reason to kick them out.

The result is we have small hearts. In fact, as time passed our hearts grew smaller and smaller.

Praise is an important weapon in the war room of prayer because it makes our hearts bigger – we understand who God is and what He can do.

Praise opens our heart to God. Praise connects us with the Everlasting Father. Praise pulls us out of our little world and gives us the bigger picture of God's sovereign kingdom.

When I start my prayer with praise, it sounds something like this:

Heavenly Father. I praise you. You are good. You are strong. You are our deliverer. You are the Everlasting One. You set a table before us. You lead us to green pastors. There is none like you. Awesome in all your deeds. Your hand is

*not too short to save. You have loved us with
an everlasting love.*

This is an example of a prayer of praise. Practice praising God in prayer until you feel your heart is bigger and you see God in His splendor. I use this hand motion to remind myself which part of prayer I am doing.

After you spend time praising God, move to the next weapon of powerful prayer: repentance.

REPENT

*If you find your life of prayer to be always
so short, and so easy, and so spiritual, as to
be without cost and strain and sweat to you,
you may depend upon it, you have not yet
begun to pray.*

— ALEXANDER WHYTE

The second weapon of powerful prayer is repentance. I've noticed when I praise God with all my heart, I become more aware of my sin. When I see holy God, I also see my faults.

Feelings of inadequacy, fears, struggles, and other difficulties rise from my heart. In fact, I question whether I am praising God with all of my heart if this doesn't happen!

How do you deal with those negative thoughts and feelings? Jesus shared a parable about two different ways people deal with their sin in Luke 18:9-14:

> Jesus told a story to some people who thought they were better than others and who looked down on everyone else:
>
> Two men went into the temple to pray. One was a Pharisee and the other a tax collector. The Pharisee stood over by himself and prayed, "God, I thank you that I am not greedy, dishonest, and unfaithful in marriage like other people. And I am really glad that I am not like that tax collector over there. I go without eating for two days a week, and I give you one tenth of all I earn."
>
> The tax collector stood off at a distance and did not think he was good enough even to look up toward heaven. He was so sorry for what he had done that he pounded his chest and prayed, "God, have pity on me! I am such a sinner."
>
> Then Jesus said, "When the two men went home, it was the tax collector and not the Pharisee

who was pleasing to God. If you put yourself above others, you will be put down. But if you humble yourself, you will be honored."

(CEV)

Some people don't deal with their sin when they pray. Instead, they think about their good deeds and the bad deeds of others. Psychologists call this misdirection. The Phariseein Jesus' parable hardened his heart by judging others.

Throughout the Bible, God cautions He will not listen to a hard-hearted person.

People like the tax collector choose to repent of their sins – owning their faults. Repenting means to admit our sin openly, feel remorse, and turn away from committing it again. This is what the tax collector did, and Jesus said he went home justified – God had heard his prayer. Repenting pleases God and connects us with His heart when we pray.

People are uncomfortable with the idea we will all face a judgment day. We feel like we are barely keeping up with our lives as it is and rationalize that God will overlook our sin. We spurn judgment day because our hearts are stubborn. We don't want to admit our wrongdoing and come up with flimsy excuses to explain it away. Comparing ourselves with others is how we usually do this. We say, "I'm not like ISIS, or people who riot, or..."

When God brings up the truth of my sin, I have two choices: I can repent or I can harden my heart. Repentance is a powerful prayer weapon in the war room, because our hearts are hard and need to be soft towards God.

When I pray the "repent" part of my prayers, I talk to God saying:

> *Lord, forgive me for my anger and how I treated my friend yesterday. I was thinking selfishly and pushing my agenda. I hurt her, and I am sorry. I could tell you were displeased and you have convicted me several times since then, but I haven't cared and have hardened my heart. Please forgive me and help me as I apologize to my friend today. Soften my heart towards you and her. I repent of my sin.*

Your prayer will be different, but I wanted to provide an example. Here is the "repent" hand motion.

After spending time repenting of your sins and softening your heart before God, move to the third weapon of powerful prayer: asking.

This is an excerpt from Dr. Lancaster's bestselling book – *Powerful Prayers in the War Room*.

MORE FROM THIS AUTHOR

POWERFUL JESUS — IN THE — **WAR ROO**
DANIEL B LANCASTER PhD

POWERFUL PRAYERS — IN THE — **WAR ROOM**
DANIEL B LANCASTER PhD

POWERFUL WORSHIP — IN THE — **AR ROOM**
DANIEL B LANCASTER PhD

#1 Best Sellers
on
amazon

This series on powerful prayer, heart-felt worship, and intimacy with Christ will help strengthen your "War Room" and give you a battle plan for prayer.

Visit go.lightkeeperbooks.com/battleplan
to learn more.

CHRISTIAN SELF-HELP

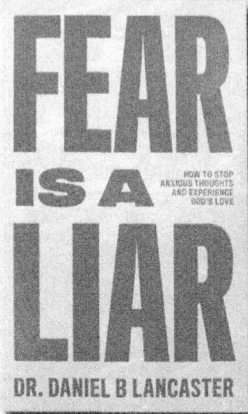

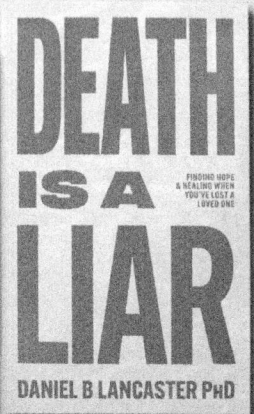

FEAR IS A LIAR
HOW TO STOP ANXIOUS THOUGHTS AND EXPERIENCE GOD'S LOVE

DR. DANIEL B LANCASTER

SHAME IS A LIAR
HOW TO SAY YES TO GOD AND NO TO SHAME

DANIEL B LANCASTER PhD

DEATH IS A LIAR
FINDING HOPE & HEALING WHEN YOU'VE LOST A LOVED ONE

DANIEL B LANCASTER PhD

Available on
amazon

Overcome fear, shame, and other spiritual attacks
that hold you back from being all God created you to be.

Visit go.lightkeeperbooks.com/selfhelp to learn more

Coming Soon

SATAN IS A LIAR
Satan only cares about himself and stopping you.
Learn how to overcome the greatest narcissist of all time.

Lightkeeper Kids Series

JOURNEY
LEARNS TO PRAY

HENRY LEARNS
TO PRAY

EVIE LEARNS
TO PRAY

FELIPE LEARNS
TO PRAY

LEARNS
PRAY

Available On
amazon

"Very sweet! Easy for kids to
understand and relate to!"

Visit go.lightkeeperbooks.com/lkk
to learn more

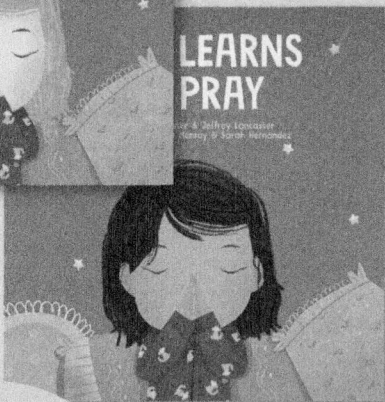

ABOUT THE AUTHOR

Daniel B Lancaster (PhD) enjoys training others to become passionate followers of Christ. He has planted two churches in America and trained over 5,000 people in Southeast Asia as a strategy coordinator with the International Mission Board. He served as Assistant Vice-President for University Ministries at Union University and currently is a international missionary with Cornerstone International. He has four grown children and a delightful grandson.

Dr. Dan is available for speaking and training events. Contact him at dan@lightkeeperbooks. com to arrange a meeting for your group.

Printed in Great Britain
by Amazon

10454765R00048